CIRIA C698

Site handbook for the construction of SUDS

B Woods Ballard   HR Wallingford
R Kellagher   HR Wallingford
P Martin   Black and Veatch
C Jefferies   University of Abertay
R Bray   Robert Bray Associates
P Shaffer   CIRIA

sharing knowledge
building best practice

Classic House, 174–180 Old Street, London EC1V 9BP
Telephone +44 (0)20 7549 3300
Fax +44 (0)20 7253 0523
Email enquiries@ciria.org
Website www.ciria.org

Site handbook for the construction of SUDS

Woods Ballard, B; Kellagher, P; Martin, P; Jefferies, C; Bray, R; Shaffer, P.

CIRIA

CIRIA C698   © CIRIA 2007   RP697   ISBN-13 978-0-86017-698-5

ISBN-10 0-86017-698-3

Keywords	
Urban drainage, climate change, flooding, environmental good practice, rivers and waterways, pollution prevention, sustainable construction, sustainable resource use, water quality, urban hydrogeology, urban regeneration, water infrastructure, rivers and waterways.	
Reader interest	**Classification**	
Developers, landscape architects, consulting engineers, local authorities, architects, highway authorities, environmental regulators, planners, sewerage undertakers and other organisations involved in the provision and maintenance of surface water drainage to new and existing developments.	AVAILABILITY	Unrestricted
	CONTENT	Guidance/advice
	STATUS	Committee-guided
	USERS	Planners, developers, engineers, regulators.

This publication is designed to provide accurate and authoritative information on the subject matter covered. It is sold and/or distributed with the understanding that neither the authors nor the publisher is thereby engaged in rendering a specific legal or any other professional service. While every effort has been made to ensure the accuracy and completeness of the publication, no warranty or fitness is provided or implied, and the authors and publisher shall have neither liability nor responsibility to any person or entity with respect to any loss or damage arising from its use.

All rights reserved. No part of this publication may be reproduced or transmitted in any form or by any means, including photocopying and recording, without the written permission of the copyright-holder, application for which should be addressed to the publisher. Such written permission must also be obtained before any part of this publication is stored in a retrieval system of any nature.

If you would like to reproduce any of the figures, text or technical information from this or any other CIRIA publication for use in other documents or publications, please contact the Publishing Department for more details on copyright terms and charges at: publishing@ciria.org Tel: 020 7549 3300.

Acknowledgements

Research contractor

This guidance has been produced as part of CIRIA Research Project 697. The detailed research was carried out by HR Wallingford Ltd, Black and Veatch, University of Abertay and CIRIA

Authors

Bridget Woods Ballard MA MSc DIC CEng MICE MCIWEM
Bridget is a principal engineer at HR Wallingford. She has more than 15 years' experience in hydrology and sustainable flood risk management and has been a key contributor to recent SUDS research on system costs, maintenance and performance for both government and the water industry.

Richard Kellagher BEng MSc CEng MICE MCIWEM
Richard is a technical director of HR Wallingford. He has been involved in drainage and SUDS research and has produced a number of guidance documents on drainage related issues for both CIRIA and HR Wallingford. His experience in drainage also includes sewerage modelling and auditing, master plans for cities overseas and leading a number of European research projects.

Peter Martin BSc MBA CEng FICE MCIWEM MCMI
Peter is operations director at Black & Veatch Ltd and has more 25 years' practical experience of the design and construction wastewater and drainage projects in the UK and overseas. He was the principal author of the original suite of CIRIA SUDS manuals. In addition, he managed the UK elements of the joint UKWIR/WERF research project Performance and Whole Life Costs of BMPs and SUDS.

Chris Jefferies BSc MSc PhD CEng MICE MCIWEM
Professor of Environmental Engineering and Head of Urban Water Technology Centre at the University of Abertay Dundee, Chris has more than 30 years' experience designing, researching and training in urban drainage. He has co-authored a range of reports on the performance and maintenance of SUDS.

Robert Bray MLI BSc (Hons) DipLD
A director of Robert Bray Associates, Bob has designed SUDS schemes since 1996 and has recently designed SUDS for schools, housing and public open space. He is co-author of *Sustainable drainage systems – hydraulic, structural and water quality advice* (CIRIA C609) and *The operation and maintenance of sustainable drainage infrastructure and associated costs* (HR Wallingford report SR 626).

Paul Shaffer BSc (Hons)

Paul is an associate at CIRIA and for 10 years has encouraged and implemented the sustainable use and management of water in the built environment. He has been responsible for a number of projects to help overcome barriers to the sustainable management of water.

CIRIA manager

CIRIA's project manager was Paul Shaffer

Contributors

CIRIA wishes to acknowledge the following individuals who provided substantial additional information for the case studies.

Aidan Millerick	Micro Drainage
Simon Bamford	Land & Water Remediation Ltd/British Waterways.

Contents

1	Introduction to SUDS	9
2	How SUDS differ from conventional drainage	10
3	General construction issues associated with SUDS	12
4	Construction planning	14
5	Erosion	18
6	Sediment control	19
7	Pollution control	20
8	Inspections	22
9	Method statements	23
10	Emergency contacts	24
11	SUDS components	25
	11.1 Pre-treatment systems	25
	11.2 Green roofs	26
	11.3 Soakaways	28
	11.4 Rainwater harvesting	29
	11.5 Filter strips	30
	11.6 Trenches	32
	11.7 Swales	33
	11.8 Bioretention	35
	11.9 Pervious pavements	36
	11.10 Geocellular systems	38
	11.11 Sand filters	40
	11.12 Infiltration basins	41
	11.13 Detention basins	42
	11.14 Ponds	43
	11.15 Wetlands	45
12	References	47
Appendices		
	A1 Erosion control	49
	A2 Sediment control	52
Glossary		54
Abbreviations		62

Figures

Figure 3.1	Earthworks on a SUDS site	13
Figure 4.1	Completed swale	17
Figure 7.1	Construction of a swale	20
Figure 11.1	Typical cross-section through a green roof system	28
Figure 11.2	Typical cross-section of a soakaway	29
Figure 11.3	Schematic view of a generic rainwater harvesting system	30
Figure 11.4	Typical cross-section through a filter strip	31
Figure 11.5	A filter trench under construction	33
Figure 11.6	A swale under construction	34
Figure 11.7	Typical cross-section through a bio-retention facility	36
Figure 11.8	Typical cross-section through a pervious pavement	38
Figure 11.9	Example of proprietary geocellular system under construction	39
Figure 11.10	Typical cross-section through a sand filter	40
Figure 11.11	Typical cross-section through an infiltration basin	42
Figure 11.12	A detention basin schematic	43
Figure 11.13	A pond under construction	44
Figure 11.14	A wetland after initial planting	45

Introduction to SUDS 1

Sustainable Drainage Systems (SUDS) are drainage systems designed to contribute to the achievement of sustainable development. Rather than traditional pipe and sewer arrangements, the philosophy of SUDS is to replicate as closely as possible the natural drainage from a site before development.

They aim to mimic natural drainage from an undeveloped situation, where rainfall soaks into the ground and saturates soil and vegetation before significant runoff occurs. The systems are designed both to manage the environmental risks resulting from urban runoff and to contribute wherever possible to environment enhancement.

SUDS elements are generally small scale and relatively shallow. They usually require the use of only fairly simple civil engineering construction and landscaping operations, such as excavation, filling, grading, topsoiling, seeding and planting. These operations are specified in various standard construction documents, such as the Civil Engineering Specification for the Water Industry (CESWI, WRc, 1998).

The performance and operation of SUDS depend upon careful planning and implementation during the construction phase, because there are some specific considerations that require changes to conventional construction practices. The use of inappropriate plant, failure to protect the system from construction runoff and detritus, and a lack of integration of landscaping with construction, can all be the cause of poor performance SUDS.

This handbook provides readily accessible guidance for easy reference and use on site. The CIRIA publication, *The SUDS Manual* (C697), provides more detailed guidance for owners, developers, planners, designers, contractors, managers and operators.

2 How SUDS differs from conventional drainage

Appropriately designed, constructed and maintained SUDS are more sustainable than conventional drainage methods because they can mitigate many of the adverse effects of urban stormwater runoff on the environment. They achieve this through:

- controlling run-off rates and volumes, thereby lessening the risk of downstream flooding
- reducing pollutant concentrations, thereby protecting downstream water bodies
- encouraging natural groundwater recharge (where appropriate)
- contributing to the enhanced amenity and aesthetic value of developed areas
- providing habitats for wildlife in urban areas and opportunities for biodiversity enhancements.

As they are intended to mimic nature, the construction and landscaping techniques required are generally simple. However, it is important to realise that the SUDS principles described above need to apply to the construction phase as much as the finished product.

Therefore, from a construction viewpoint, SUDS require that specific attention is given to:

1. The planning and phasing of construction to ensure that the performance of the facilities is not compromised by over compaction or clogging with construction debris for example. Please refer to the section on general construction issues associated with SUDS in this handbook.
2. Construction planning taking account of programming and erosion, sediment and pollution control measures, together with the need for method statements and inspections by the designer. Please refer to the sections on construction planning, inspections and method statements.
3. Erosion which will reduce the effectiveness of SUDS facilities, and add to the silt load that any other drainage feature downstream will have to deal with. Please refer to the section on erosion, which addresses both erosion control procedures and erosion protection techniques.

4. Sediment entrapment facilities which are necessary to reduce sediment discharges to downstream properties and receiving waters. Please refer to the section on sediment control.

5. Surface water runoff and pumped water from construction sites which must not pollute receiving waters. Please refer to the section on pollution control.

3 General construction issues associated with SUDS

- The planning of temporary drainage during the construction phase is critical both to the success of SUDS and to the avoidance of pollution downstream. Silt-laden waters from construction sites are one of the most common forms of waterborne pollution.

- Runoff from the construction site must not be allowed to enter SUDS drainage systems unless it has been allowed for in the design and specification. Construction runoff is heavily laden with silt, which can clog infiltration systems, build up in storage systems and pollute receiving waters.

- Normally, drainage is an early activity in construction. For SUDS, although the form of the drainage will be constructed during the earthworks phase, the final construction should not take place until the end of site development work, unless adequate provision is made to remove any silt that is deposited during construction operations.

- All inlets and outlets should be carefully constructed, taking account of all design details. Inlet systems should spread the flow and must avoid scouring of soil or other material from surfaces. Outlets will tend to be smaller than inlets forcing water to be stored within the drainage system.

- Careful levelling and grading is crucial to the performance of many SUDS features to ensure that water flows through the system without ponding – which can damage vegetation and cause unattractive muddy zones to develop. In particular, grass filter strips and swales must be lower than the impermeable surfaces that they drain.

- Before runoff is allowed to flow through SUDS techniques with surface-formed features such as swales, they must be fully stabilised by planting or temporary erosion protection. This will prevent erosion of the sides and base, and the clogging of other parts of the system by the silt that is entrained.

- Car parking and other paved areas are usually constructed (or partially constructed) during the initial stages of the development, and then used as access roads and storage areas. If pervious surfaces are specified in the SUDS, pavement construction should be carried out at the end of the development programme, unless adequate protection is provided to preventing clogging or blinding once it has been constructed. The storage of soil or subsoil on the surfaces of permeable systems (including filter drains) will destroy their function.

- Construction planning, therefore, needs to take account of the programming and erosion, sediment and pollution control measures, together with the need for inspections by the designer to confirm acceptability.
- Provision should have been made in the construction contract to review the performance of the SUDS when it is completed, and to allow for minor adjustments and refinements to be made to optimise the physical arrangements, based on observed performance. Such adjustments are likely to have to be made late in the construction phase, or in the maintenance period.

Figure 3.1 *Earthworks on a SUDS site*

4 Construction planning

Construction planning needs to take account of the programming and erosion, sediment and pollution control measures, together with the need for inspections.

The features requiring particular attention during the construction phase are: site access, storage of materials, site drainage during construction, and protection of surfaces from erosion, sedimentation or overcompaction.

Construction programming considerations are summarised below. The generalised construction activities shown in the table do not usually occur in a specified linear sequence, and programmes will vary due to season, weather and other unpredictable factors.

Construction activity	Programme consideration
Identify and sign protection areas (eg buffer zones, filter strips, trees).	Site delineation should be completed before any construction activity begins.
Construction access, construction entrance, construction routes, equipment parking areas and cutting of vegetation (with any necessary boundary controls).	The first land-disturbing activity. Establish protected areas. Stabilise bare areas and provide temporary protection as construction takes place.
Sediment traps and barriers. Basin traps, sediment fences, and outlet protection (with any necessary boundary controls).	Install principal basins after construction site is accessed. Install additional traps and barriers as needed during grading.
Runoff control. Diversions, silt fence, perimeter ditches and outlet protection.	Install key measures after principal sediment traps have been installed and before grading begins. Install any additional runoff control measures during grading.
Runoff conveyance system. Stabilise stream banks, storm drains, channels, inlet and outlet protection, and slope drains.	Where necessary, stabilise stream banks as early as possible. Install principal runoff conveyance system with runoff control measures. Install remainder of system after grading.
Clearing and grading. Site preparation: traps, barriers, diversions, drains, surface treatment.	Begin major clearing and grading after principal sediment and key runoff control measures are installed. Clear borrow and disposal areas only as needed. Install additional control measures as grading progresses.
Surface stabilisation: temporary and permanent seeding, mulching, topsoiling and installing riprap.	Apply temporary or permanent stabilisation measures immediately on all disturbed areas where work is either delayed or complete.
Building construction: buildings, utilities and paving.	Install necessary erosion and sedimentation control practices as work takes place.
Landscaping and final stabilisation: topsoiling, planting trees and shrubs, permanent seeding, mulching, installing riprap.	The last construction phase. Stabilise all open areas, including borrow and spoil areas. Remove and stabilise all temporary control measures.
Commissioning and pre-handover maintenance	Maintenance inspections should be performed weekly, and maintenance repairs should be made immediately after periods of rainfall.

Points to consider:

- Construction access: care should be taken not to damage valuable trees or disturb designated buffer zones. Trees should be protected around the drip line of the branches. Activities that could compact the root zone should be avoided.
- Sediment basins and traps should be installed before any major site grading takes place. Additional sediment traps and silt fences should be installed as grading takes place to keep sediment contained on site at appropriate locations.
- Key runoff control measures should be located in conjunction with sediment traps to divert water from planned undisturbed areas away from the traps and sediment-laden water into the traps. Diversions should be installed above areas to be disturbed before any grading operations. Any perimeter drains should be installed with stable outlets before opening major areas for development. Any additional facilities needed for runoff control should be installed as grading takes place.
- The main runoff conveyance system with inlet and outlet protection measures should be installed early, and used to convey stormwater runoff through the development site without creating gullies or channels. Install inlet protection for storm drains (as soon as the drain is functional) to trap sediment on site in shallow pools and to allow flood flows to enter the storm drainage system safely. Install outlet protection at the same time as the conveyance system to prevent damage to the receiving stream.
- Normally, install stream stabilisation, including necessary stream crossings, independently and ahead of other construction activities. It is usually best to programme this work as soon as weather conditions permit. Site clearing and project construction increases storm runoff, often making stream-bank-stabilisation work more difficult and costly.
- Begin clearing and grading as soon as key erosion and sediment control measures are in place. Once a development area is cleared, grading should follow immediately so that protective ground cover can be re-established quickly. Do not leave any area bare and exposed for extended periods. Leave adjoining areas planned for development, or those that are to be used for borrow and disposal, undisturbed as long as possible to serve as natural buffer zones.
- Runoff control is essential during the grading operation. Temporary diversions, slope drains, and inlet and outlet protection installed in a timely manner can be very effective in controlling erosion during this critical period of development.

- After the land is cleared and graded, apply surface stabilisation on graded areas, channels, ditches and other disturbed areas. Stabilise any disturbed area where active construction will not take place for 60 working days, by temporary seeding and/or mulching or by other suitable means. Install permanent stabilisation measures as soon as possible after final grading. Temporary seeding and/or mulching may be necessary during extreme weather conditions with permanent vegetation measures delayed until a more suitable installation time.

- Coordinate building construction with other development activities so that all work can take place in an orderly manner and on programme. Experience shows that careful project programming improves efficiency, reduces cost and lowers the potential for erosion and sedimentation problems.

- Landscaping and final stabilisation is the last major construction phase, but topsoil stockpiling, tree preservation, undisturbed buffer areas, and well-planned road locations established earlier in the project may determine the ease or difficulty of this activity. All disturbed areas should have permanent stabilisation measures applied. Unstable sediment should be removed from sediment basins and traps and if possible incorporated into the topsoil, not just spread on the surface. All temporary structures should be removed after the area above has been properly stabilised. Borrow and disposal areas should be permanently vegetated or otherwise stabilised.

- In planning construction work, it may be helpful to outline all land-disturbing activities necessary to complete the proposed project. Then list all practices needed to control erosion and sedimentation on the site. These two lists can then be combined in a logical order to provide a practical and effective construction programme.

Figure 4.1   *Completed swale*

- When construction is finished, there is likely to be a commissioning period in which the permanent SUDS are made "live", this is likely to include diversion of drainage flows into the new facilities. If permanent facilities have been used wholly or in part to drain the site, or as other forms of temporary works such as roads or storage areas, then there may be rehabilitation works required to reconstitute or restore them to their design condition. Once the permanent facilities have been demonstrated to work as envisaged, temporary drainage and sediment and erosion control measures can be carefully dismantled so as not to generate sediment loading on downstream systems.

5 Erosion

Erosion control is needed to limit the amount and rate of erosion occurring on disturbed areas. Erosion of SUDS components will reduce their effectiveness. Erosion generally will add to the silt load that any other drainage feature downstream will have to deal with. Erosion controls are surface treatments that stabilise soil exposed by excavation or grading.

Details of erosion control and erosion protection techniques are provided in Appendix 1.

Site assessment
The following guidelines are recommended in developing the erosion and sediment control elements during the planning phase:
♦ **Determine the limits of clearing and grading.** If the entire site does not need to undergo excavation and grading, the boundaries of cut and fill operations should be defined. Retaining buffer strips of natural vegetation should be considered.
♦ **Define the layout of buildings and roads.** This will have been decided previously as a part of the general development plan.
♦ **Determine permanent drainage features.** The location of permanent channels, surface water sewers, roadside swales and quality controls such as ponds, wetlands, grassed-lined swales, buffer strips, and areas of porous pavement, if known, should be defined.
♦ **Determine the extent of any temporary channel diversions.** If permanent channel improvements are a part of the plan, the route, sizing, and lining needed for temporary channel diversions should be determined. Location and type of temporary channel crossings can be assessed.
♦ **Determine the boundaries of drainage catchments.** The size will determine the types of sediment controls to be used. Areas located off the site that contribute to overland flow runoff must be assessed. Measures to limit the size of upland overland flow areas, such as diversion ditches, will need to be considered.
♦ **Select sediment controls.** The division of large drainage catchments into sub-areas each served by a sediment basin can also be considered.
♦ **Determine the staging of construction.** The construction programme will determine what areas must be disturbed at various stages throughout the development plan. The opportunity for staging cut-and-fill operations to minimise the period of exposure of soils can be assessed. The sequence for installing sediment controls and erosion controls should also be determined.
♦ **Identify locations of topsoil stockpiles.** Areas for storing topsoil should be determined.
♦ **Identify location of temporary construction roads, vehicle tracking controls, and material storage areas.**
♦ **Select erosion controls.** All areas of exposed soil will require a control measure to be defined dependent on the duration of exposure. These can be selected based on the construction programme.

Sediment control 6

Sediment entrapment facilities are necessary to reduce sediment discharges to downstream properties and receiving waters.

Details of sediment control are provided in Appendix B.

7 Pollution control

Guidance on prevention of pollution during construction is provided in the following publications:

- *Control of water pollution from construction sites – guide to good practice*, C532 (CIRIA, 2001)
- *Guide to good practice on site*, SP156 (CIRIA 2002)
- *Control of water pollution from linear construction projects. Technical guidance*, C648 (CIRIA 2006)
- *Control of water pollution from linear construction projects. Site guide*, C649 (CIRIA 2006)

Further guidance can be found in the pollution prevention guidelines produced by the Environment Agency and SEPA. Following this guidance should help prevent damage to SUDS techniques during construction.

The main requirements are to control surface water runoff and pumped water from sites – for example by the use of settling tanks – to ensure that sediments and chemicals do not pollute receiving waters. The safe storage of materials and fuels is also important so that if spills occur they are contained (by the use of berms, check ditches or other techniques) and do not cause a pollution incident. Although it is worth emphasising that sediments in suspension are the most common form of pollution.

Before mobilisation, the site layout should be planned for issues such as the location of stockpiles, fuel stores, storage areas, waste disposal, refuelling points, wash down areas, etc. These should be located in areas where they are least likely to affect controlled waters. The planning should also address subjects such as the diversion of watercourses, prevention of upstream runoff entering the site and the design of haul roads, including the use of road bridges over watercourses to stop vehicles fording streams and rivers.

Figure 7.1
Construction of a swale

An environmental plan should also be put in place. The plan should include: an environmental risk assessment with control measures; location of foul drainage disposal routes; location of surface water systems that discharge into watercourses; requirements for discharge and abstraction licences; location of spillage kits and an action plan in the event of an environmental incident (including a list of relevant telephone contact numbers).

The following list indicates a number of sources of potential pollution and the measure that can be taken to help manage risks:
♦ **Excavated ground and exposed ground.** The effect of having no vegetation and being recently disturbed allows for relatively low velocity run-off to erode the surface. To help prevent the pollution from entering a watercourse, silt fences, straw bales or stilling ponds should be placed downstream. To limit the volume of run-off reaching the exposed ground, runoff diversion or interception devices should be placed upstream.
♦ **Stockpiles.** The effects of erosion on a stockpile will depend on the type of material being stored. Fine sand and topsoil stockpiles will be eroded far more readily than heavy granular materials. Stockpiles should be located away from a watercourse or site drainage system. Protective coverings will help prevent runoff stripping the stockpile.
♦ **Plant and wheel washing.** Plant and wheel washing should take place in designated locations. The area should be tanked and should not be allowed to discharge into a watercourse, or infiltrate the ground, as the wastewater from these devices is highly contaminated with silts, sands, and hydrocarbons. Some proprietary vehicle washing systems offer a recycling facility, which filter and settle solids, with the effluent being pumped back into the system. The solid waste materials from this process need to be treated as contaminated waste due to the high hydrocarbon content.
♦ **Haul roads.** The runoff from haul roads contains large amounts of suspended solids as well as hydrocarbons. Haul roads should be designed so that the length is kept to a minimum, but still serves its purpose. The gradient should be shallow to prevent increasing runoff velocity and, if possible, bunds and/or discrete ditches constructed to intercept the runoff. Haul roads should be watered on a regular basis to keep dust down. If any sections of haul roads are hard surfaced they should be cleaned on a regular basis to prevent the accumulation of dust and mud.
♦ **Disturbance of riverbeds or banks.** Excavation of riverbanks or beds can generate silty water as the excavated and exposed material is washed downstream. The amount of such excavation needs to be limited and, if undertaken, the water area downstream needs to be protected by booms. For larger projects, consideration should be given to diverting the river while excavation takes place.

♦ **Dewatering operations.** Groundwater discharge is likely to be heavily polluted with suspended solids and should not be discharged directly into a watercourse. To help reduce the amount of suspended solids within the runoff a number of techniques can be adopted:
  – passing the discharge water over a grass area, the discharge velocity has to be monitored and kept sufficiently low to promote settlement
  – passing the discharge water though a temporary gravel strip
  – controlled use of skips and/or tanks to act as stilling basins
  – controlled use of stilling ponds.

♦ **Concrete washout areas.** Where it is required to clean out concrete wagons or skips containing wet concrete mixes a designated area should be made available clear of watercourses or drainage systems so that the cement content does not enter water systems or block or blind drainage networks. This area may require an impermeable surfacing to prevent seepage into underlying soils.

8 Inspections

Inspection of the construction of a SUDS scheme should be carried out to ensure that the system is being constructed correctly, and that design assumptions and criteria are not invalidated, for example, by the construction methods used, by changes made on site or by variations in ground conditions.

The form of inspection will depend upon the type of construction contract used. Typically, either self-certification by the contractor or supervisory inspection by the designer.

These inspections should be undertaken as necessary, but as a minimum would generally be expected to include the following:

- pre-excavation inspection to ensure that construction runoff is being adequately dealt with on site and will not cause clogging of the SUDS components
- inspections of excavations for ponds, infiltration devices, swales, etc
- inspections during laying of any pipework
- inspections and testing during the placing of earthworks materials or filter materials
- inspection of the prepared SUDS component before planting begins
- inspection of completed planting
- final inspection before handover to client.

The contractor installing the SUDS scheme should be made fully aware of the requirements for inspections, to avoid work being undertaken that cannot be validated.

9 Method statements

The implementation of a comprehensive Quality Assessment regime is fundamental to the achievement of a minimum standard of workmanship. It is generally accepted that a high proportion of the perceived failures of SUDS components are as a direct result of either poor quality workmanship at the installation stage or damage during construction.

Correct construction of SUDS is of equal importance as design if they are to be successfully implemented, and the key to this is conveying information to site staff (management and operatives). They need to be aware of how the SUDS scheme operates, the design requirements and how their actions on site can affect the final performance of the scheme. It is important to ensure that all sub-contractors and their operatives are involved in and engaged this process.

Site staff and operatives need to be advised how and where to install critical items, for example where geotextiles and geomembranes are to be placed in the construction. *In one case, an impermeable geomembrane was placed in a pervious surface in place of the geotextile – with the obvious consequences.* This can be viewed as an extreme example, but clogging, blinding or over-compaction of permeable surfaces due to ill-considered construction activities are likely to be more common.

The preparation and dissemination of appropriately detailed method statements emphasising the differences from traditional construction activities is an important communication channel, to be used in conjunction with tool-box talks, and direct briefings to operatives. Equally, if site staff are unsure about the specification or detailing of some features, they should consult the designer for clarification. **If in doubt, ask!**

10 Emergency contacts

Method statements and construction plans should provide local contact details (names, telephone numbers and out-of-hours contact details), and who should contact them, for the following organisations:

- client
- designer
- regulator (Environment Agency, Scottish Environmental Protection Agency or Northern Ireland Environment and Heritage Service)
- water and sewerage company
- local council
- emergency services
- neighbours
- any other stakeholders.

The emergency contact number for the UK environmental regulators is 0800 80 70 60

SUDS components 11

The following pages provide an outline of various SUDS components, and details of specific construction points to be noted for that particular technique. They are intended to be read in conjunction with the general sections on construction planning and programming, erosion control, sediment control and pollution control.

CIRIA publication *SUDS manual – guidance on design and construction* (C697) provides more detailed guidance for owners, developers, planners, designers, contractors, managers and operators on each of the various SUDS components detailed in the following pages.

◆ pre-treatment systems	◆ wetlands	◆ sand filters
◆ green roofs	◆ bioretention	◆ pervious pavements
◆ soakaways	◆ trenches	◆ detention basins
◆ rainwater harvesting	◆ swales	◆ geocellular systems
◆ ponds	◆ filter strips	◆ infiltration basins

11.1 Pre-treatment systems

The purpose of pre-treatment is to remove silt, sediment and debris from runoff prior to discharge to a downstream SUDS component. Pre-treatment options are intended to prevent clogging and reduce the need for maintenance of the downstream treatment facility. Easy access for maintenance equipment is required to remove the sediment that will be concentrated in the device. Further detail on pre-treatment systems can be found in *The SUDS Manual* (C697).

CIRIA C698 25

Pre-treatment component	Description
Vegetated buffers (filter strips)	These are vegetated strips of land over which flows are treated at low velocities. They are appropriate as pre-treatment devices for SUDS components receiving sheet flow from adjacent impervious areas eg filter drains, swales, permeable pavements.
Dry swales	These are vegetated channels over which flows are treated at low velocities. They can be used as pre-treatment devices for SUDS components receiving point source inflows.
Detention basins	These remove settleable solids from runoff by gravitational processes. Runoff enters the basin via an energy dissipating inlet structure and is allowed to spread out. The water is then conveyed to the next treatment stage via a raised outlet pipe, or other conveyance method. Detention basins are also often used as temporary measures to minimise the escape of settleable solids from temporarily disturbed land such as construction sites or quarries.
Sediment sumps	These structures retain a permanent pool of water. They reduce flow velocities and allow larger particles to settle out, by gravitational separation. They may be located above or below ground and may be contained within the treatment facility or within a separate structure. Commonly used types of sediment sumps include forebays and sedimentation manholes.
Vortex separators	These structures promote settling and collection of sediments and other pollutants. With appropriate maintenance, they can demonstrate high removal rates for coarse material, but they do not remove finer particles.
Proprietary filtration systems	These systems filter water by passing it through various filter media. Their appropriateness and likely performance should be evaluated for site-specific applications. Maintenance requirements should be given full consideration in all circumstances.
Catch basin inserts	These systems can be inserted into standard curb or grate inlets and provide limited removal of sediments, debris, oil and grease from road runoff.
Oil separators	Oil/water separators are applicable for treating surface water runoff from areas where hydrocarbon products are handled (eg petrol stations, storage areas, lorry parks, airports etc), or where small oil spills regularly fall on paved surfaces exposed to rain. They require ongoing maintenance to ensure effective operation.

Where pre-treatment units are prefabricated, construction concerns generally relate to the following:

1. Compaction of foundations to ensure that uneven settling will not occur.
2. Quality control of foundation levels to ensure inflow and outflow pipes are at the correct elevation.

Particular attention should be paid to manufacturers information in respect of backfilling and ballasting, and implementation of the CDM Regulations (DETR, 1994).

11.2 Green roofs

Description: Green roofs comprise a multi-layered system that covers the roof of a building or podium structure with vegetation cover/landscaping/permeable car parking, over a drainage layer. They are designed to intercept and retain precipitation, reducing the volume of runoff and attenuating peak flows.

Correct application of the waterproof membrane is essential to the viability of the green roof. Quality control must be assured through the use of certified roofing procedures and a water test immediately following membrane application to ensure impermeability.

Temporary ballasting of individual components may be required during construction to prevent uplift due to wind.

Implementation of the CDM Regulations and generic health and safety criteria is very important. Safe access is required for construction of the green roof, and also for all activities in areas beneath the roof. Ideally the roof should be installed when no follow-on trades will use the roof after installation, in order to reduce the risk of damage and consolidation.

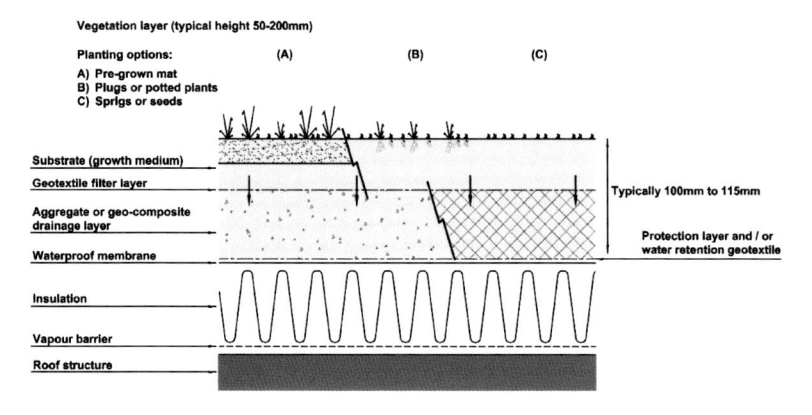

Figure 11.1 *Typical cross-section through a green roof system*

11.3 Soakaways

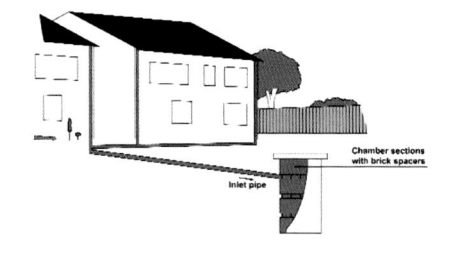

Description: Soakaways are square or circular excavations, either filled with rubble or lined with brickwork, pre-cast concrete or polyethylene rings/perforated storage structures surrounded by granular backfill. They can be grouped and linked together for large drainage areas including highways, and the supporting structure and backfill can be substituted for modular, geocellular units. Soakaways provide stormwater attenuation, stormwater treatment and groundwater recharge.

Soakaways should not be used for untreated drainage from construction sites, where runoff is likely to contain large amounts of silt, debris and other pollutants.

Perforated, pre-cast concrete ring soakaways should be installed within a square pit, with sides about twice the selected ring diameter. Oversizing the soakaway pit for purposes of constructing the ring unit chamber may be used to advantage by incorporating the total excavation volume below the discharge drain invert in the design storage volume (BRE, 1991).

Some, otherwise permeable soils and soft rocks (eg chalk), can have their permeability significantly reduced by smearing of the surface during excavation, especially by mechanical diggers.

It is recommended that the exposed surface of the soil is manually cleaned of any smearing before the geotextile and granular fill surrounding the chamber are installed.

Soakaways should always be constructed using safe construction methods and implementation of the CDM Regulations (DETR, 1994) and generic health and safety criteria is important.

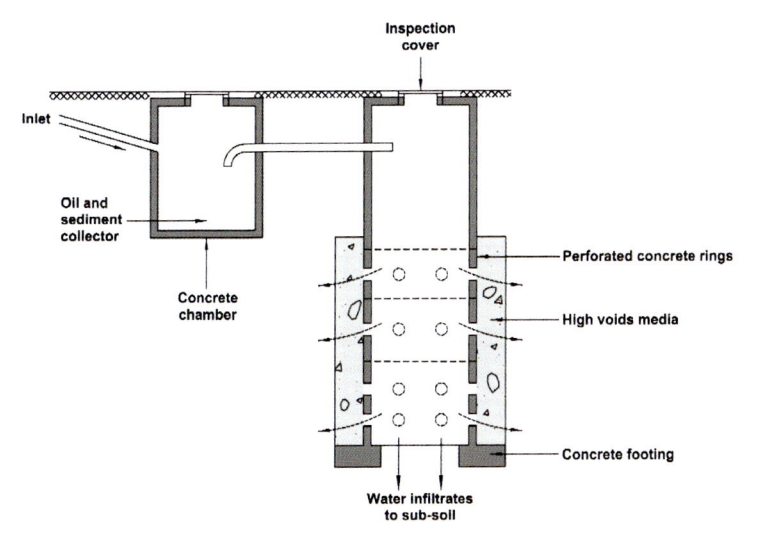

Figure 11.2   *Typical cross-section of a soakaway*

11.4 Rainwater harvesting

Description: Rainwater from roofs and hard surfaces can be stored and used. If designed appropriately, the systems can also be used to reduce the rates and volumes of runoff for small, frequent events.

Care must be taken to avoid cross-connections, and pipe marking is essential (refer to Water Supply (Water Fittings) Regulations, DETR, 1999). Chapter 2 of CIRIA publication C697 provides some material on legal issues and additional detail is provided in CIRIA C626 (Shaffer et al, 2004).

Implementation of the CDM Regulations (DETR, 1994) and generic health and safety criteria is important. Excavations for sub-surface storage tanks must be conducted safely and manufacturer's instructions for installation should always be followed.

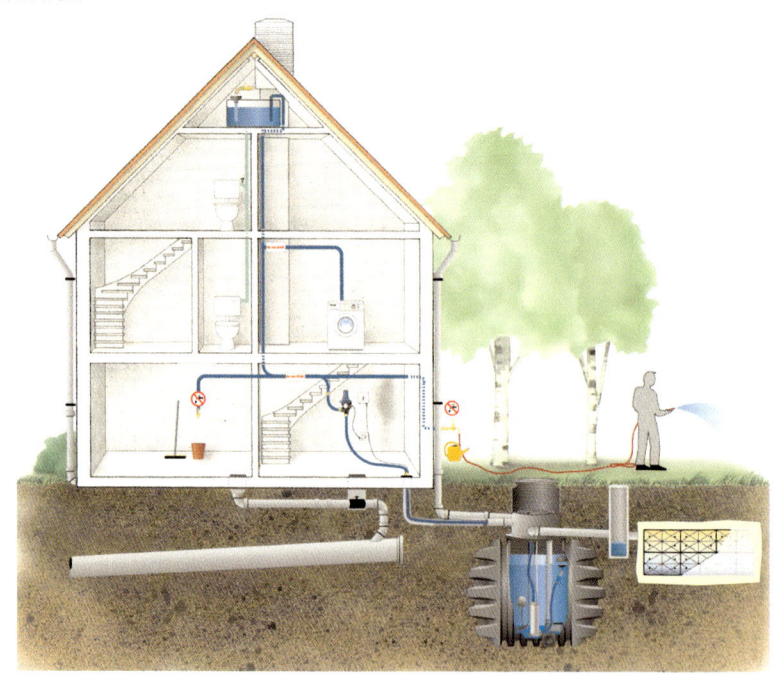

Figure 11.3 *Schematic view of a generic rainwater harvesting system*

11.5 Filter Strips

Description: Filter strips are vegetated strips of land designed to accept runoff as overland sheet flow from upstream development. They lie between a hard-surfaced area and a receiving stream, surface water collection, treatment or disposal system. They treat runoff by vegetative filtering, and promote settlement of particulate pollutants and infiltration.

11.6 Trenches

Description: Trenches are shallow excavations filled with rubble or stone that create temporary subsurface storage for either infiltration or filtration of stormwater runoff. Ideally they should receive lateral inflow from an adjacent impermeable surface, but point source inflows may be acceptable. Infiltration trenches allow water to exfiltrate into the surrounding soils from the bottom and sides of the trench. Filtration or filter trenches can be used to filter and convey stormwater to downstream SUDS components.

Trenches should be protected prior to completion and stabilisation of the upstream development areas. They should not be used for untreated drainage of construction sites, where runoff is likely to contain large amounts of silt, debris and other pollutants as this will cause rapid clogging of the systems.

The ground surrounding infiltration trenches should be left undisturbed during construction, as any trafficking of the ground or ground re-working will affect the infiltration characteristics of the soil. Geotextile and stone fill should be clean prior to construction.

Filter trench formations should be flat or to a level, shallow grade to reduce the risk of ponding and negative filter gradients.

The drain down time after a storm should be observed after completion or modification of the facility to confirm that the desired drain time has been obtained (BRE, 1991).

All trench excavations should follow construction best practice and be supported, if required. Implementation of the CDM Regulations (DETR, 1994) and generic health and safety criteria is important.

Figure 11.5 *A filter trench under construction*

11.7 Swales

Description: Swales are linear vegetated drainage features in which surface water can be stored or conveyed. They can be designed to allow infiltration, where appropriate. They should promote low flow velocities to allow much of the suspended particulate load in the stormwater runoff to settle out, thus providing effective pollutant removal. Roadside swales can replace conventional gullies and drainage pipes.

Swales should not receive any runoff until vegetation in the system is fully established and construction at the site has reached a state where sediment from the site will not cause siltation of the swale.

CIRIA C698

This can be achieved by:

(a) Diverting flows until the vegetation is well rooted;
(b) Placing an erosion control blanket (eg jute, straw or geosynthetic mats) over the freshly applied seed mix.
(c) Using bare earth as a temporary cover during the wet season. These areas should be seeded with a suitable grass mix as soon as the weather is conducive to seed germination.

If more than 30 per cent of the planted area is bare after four weeks, reseeding or replanting should be considered to achieve 90 per cent coverage. If sediment from construction work accumulates on a swale, it should be cleared and the swale fully rehabilitated before the drainage system is adopted by the organisation carrying out the maintenance.

Care must be taken that design levels and slopes for inlets and swale base and sides are constructed accurately to avoid runoff bypassing swale inlets, ponding in the swale base and flow channelling. Care should be taken not to compact the soil below a swale as this will reduce its capacity for infiltration.

Implementation of the CDM Regulations (DETR, 1994) and generic health and safety criteria is important.

Figure 11.6   *A swale under construction*

11.8 Bioretention

Description: Bioretention areas are shallow, depressed landscaped areas which are typically underdrained and rely on engineered soils and enhanced vegetation and filtration to remove pollution and reduce runoff downstream. They are principally aimed at managing frequent rainfall events.

Bioretention areas should ideally be constructed at the end of development, to minimise erosion and sediment generation, and a dense and vigorous vegetative cover should be established over the contributing pervious catchment area before runoff is accepted into the facility. If this is impractical, bioretention areas should be protected from runoff by using silt fences or straw bales as recommended in the CIRIA publication Control of water pollution from construction sites, C532 (Masters-Williams *et al*, 2001).

To minimise the risk of premature system failure the following points should be closely monitored during the construction of bioretention areas:

- care should be taken not to compact the soils below the bioretention area, and particularly the filter and soil planting bed, as this will reduce infiltration capacities
- to excavate a bioretention area, a backhoe excavator should be used and construction plant should avoid running over the bioretention area
- mulch should not be piled up around plants as this will cause disease and encourage pests
- care should be taken to ensure that geotextiles are not clogged or torn during construction
- if soil for the filter layer is imported, soil testing should be carried out, which should include a particle size distribution, pH and organic matter test for each retention area.

Implementation of the CDM Regulations (DETR, 1994) and generic health and safety criteria is important.

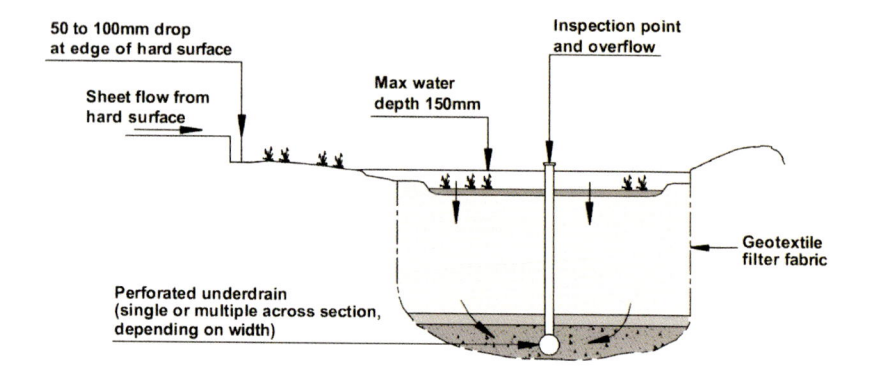

Figure 11.7 *Typical cross-section through a bio-retention facility*

11.9 Pervious pavements

Description: Pervious pavements provide a pavement suitable for pedestrian and/or vehicular traffic, whilst allowing rainwater to infiltrate through the surface and into the underlying layers. The water can then be temporarily stored prior to infiltration to the ground, re-use, or discharge to a watercourse or other drainage system. Pavements with aggregate sub-bases can provide good water quality treatment.

The following guidance should be considered when constructing a pervious pavement structure:

1. Any sub-grade soft spots should be excavated and back-filled with suitable well compacted material. The formation should be prepared by trimming to level and compacting in accordance with Specification for Highways Works, to a tolerance of +20 to −30 mm. If sub-grade improvement is employed, testing will be needed to demonstrate that the design CBR values have been consistently achieved.

2. Any impermeable membrane must be correctly specified, installed and treated with care to ensure that it is not damaged during construction.

3. The fines in a conventional impermeable material help to bind the different size particles together, and act to restrict the passage of water. In the case of permeable pavement materials which lack fines, there is potential for segregation during the transportation and construction process. Care should be taken to avoid segregation but, if this occurs, corrective action must be taken. This can be minimised by using an angular, crushed material with high surface friction.

Unlike material for conventional pavements, those for permeable pavements must not be compacted to minimise voids. This could result in surface movement when construction traffic passes over. It may be desirable to undertake site trials to determine the appropriate construction methodology.

The sub-base should be laid in 100-150 mm layers and compacted to ensure that the maximum density is achieved for the particular material type and grading, without crushing the individual particles, or reducing the void ratio below the design value, within a tolerance of +20 mm to -15 mm of the design level.

4. Geotextiles should be laid in accordance with manufacturer's instructions and with overlaps between adjacent strips of 300 mm without any folds or creases. It is recommended that specialist advice be sought from the manufacturer or supplier of the geosynthetic filter.
5. Generally, concrete block pavements should be constructed in accordance with BS 7533: Part3: 2005, Code of Practice for laying precast concrete paving blocks and clay pavers for flexible pavements, the technical sections for which are available for download on the Interpave website at www.paving.org. Advice should be sought from the specific manufacturer on any product specific requirements, laying and jointing materials, block patterns and block laying procedures. In accordance with good practice, the block surface layer should be fully compacted and jointed to within 1 m of the laying face at the end of each day. Other pavement surfaces should be constructed according to the relevant British Standards and/or the surface manufacturer's guidance.

Preventing impermeable contaminants such as soil and mud from entering the pavement surface and sub-base both during and after construction is imperative to ensure that the pavement remains permeable throughout its design life. Construction equipment should be kept away from the area and silt fences, staged excavation works and temporary drainage swales which divert runoff away from the area should all be considered to manage these risks.

Landscaping activities should be carefully designed and carried out to prevent deposition of topsoil, turf and other materials on the surface of the pavement. Infiltration surfaces must not be compacted and should be protected at all times.

Implementation of the CDM Regulations (DETR, 1994) and generic health and safety criteria is important.

Figure 11.8 *Typical cross-section through a pervious pavement*

11.10 Geocellular systems

Description: Modular plastic geocellular systems with a high void ratio that can be used to create a below ground infiltration (soakaway) or storage structure.

In addition to appropriate design, it is critical that the ground preparation and system installation are carried out to appropriate quality control conditions. Guidance should be sought from individual manufacturers on system-specific best practice.

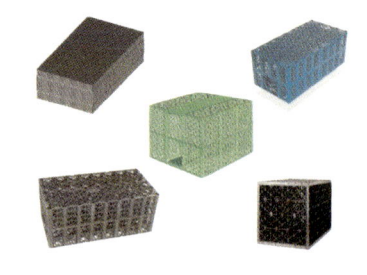

Post installation, and in untrafficked situations, excavations can generally be backfilled with selected, as-dug material that does not contain large particles or sharp materials. It should then be well compacted. In trafficked areas, the use of well compacted backfill and cover is particularly important and the material should, typically, be selected in accordance with standard highway works specifications (eg Highways Agency et al, 1996). Use of poor quality backfill can significantly increase lateral earth pressures and cause collapse. Running heavy plant over constructed tanks or stockpiling material over them during construction, when such loads have not been included within design calculations, can also cause collapse, especially if temporary cover during site works is less than the final design cover depth. Where the system is being used as a storage tank, the geomembrane wrapping may need to be protected from the backfill by a geotextile fleece in some instances.

In all cases, advice should be sought from individual manufacturers regarding specific recommended installation and cover depths.

Runoff should be prevented from entering the modular blocks during construction. Alternatively, and only if the design allows, a flushing operation may be required prior to commissioning to ensure all sediments have been removed from the system.

All storage tanks should be fully sealed in accordance with waterproofing standards (ie welded joints rather than adhesive taped) and the integrity of the seal checked through the use of non-destructive testing, to ensure it is leak-proof. Care needs to be taken during installation against damage of both the modular structure and the geotextile and/or geomembrane wrapping. Follow-on trades can also cause damage and put the integrity of the structure at risk.

Implementation of the CDM Regulations (DETR, 1994) and generic health and safety criteria is important.

Figure 11.9 *Example of proprietary geocellular system under construction*

11.11 Sand filters

Description: Sand filters are single or multi-chambered structures designed to treat surface water runoff through filtration using a sand bed as the primary filter medium. The filters can be designed with an impervious lining, or to allow infiltration, depending on the soil type. Temporary storage of runoff is achieved through ponding above the filter layer. They are used where particularly high pollutant removal is required.

Sand filters should not receive any runoff until vegetation in the system is fully established and construction at the site has reached a state where sediment concentrations in the runoff will not cause clogging. If sediment from construction work accumulates on a sand filter surface, it should be cleared and the filter fully rehabilitated before the drainage system is adopted by the organisation carrying out the maintenance.

It is important that the top of the filter bed is constructed completely level, otherwise filtration will be localised and early failure may occur.

In areas where groundwater protection is a concern, the completed tank structure (concrete or membrane) should be filled with water for 24 hours to ensure that there is no leakage.

Implementation of the CDM Regulations (DETR, 1994) and generic health and safety criteria is important.

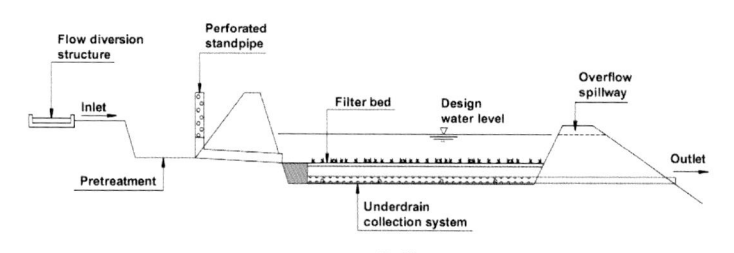

Figure 11.10 *Typical cross-section through a sand filter*

11.12 Infiltration basins

Description: Infiltration basins are vegetated depressions designed to store runoff and infiltrate it gradually into the ground.

Ideally, construction of the infiltration basin should take place after the site has been stabilised in order to minimise the risk of premature failure of the basin from deposition of sediments from disturbed ground. If this is not possible, then initial excavation should be carried out to within 450 mm of the basin floor and final excavation should be delayed until after stabilisation.

All excavation and levelling should be performed by equipment with tracks exerting very light pressures to prevent compaction of the basin floor, which may reduce infiltration capacity. Before and after construction, other vehicular movements should be prevented.

The base of the basin should be carefully prepared to an even grade with no significant undulations. The surface soils within the basin should not be smeared or compacted during construction. After final grading, the basin floor should be tilled to a depth of 150 mm to provide a well-aerated, porous surface texture.

Backfilling against inlet and outlet structures needs to be controlled to minimise settlement and erosion. The topsoils used to finish the side slopes need to be suitably fertile, porous and of sufficient depth to ensure healthy vegetation growth.

It is essential that infiltration basins should not be used to manage construction runoff and trap construction sediments.

Implementation of the CDM Regulations (DETR, 1994) and generic health and safety criteria is important.

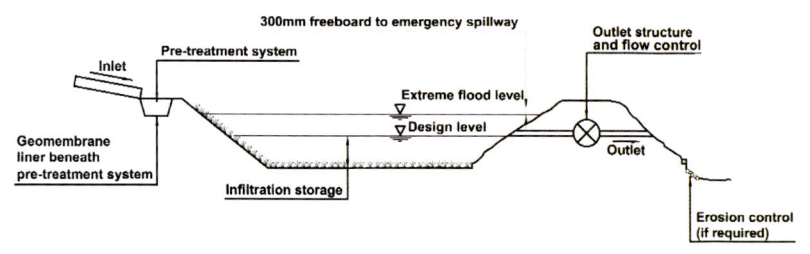

Figure 11.11 *Typical cross-section through an infiltration basin*

11.13 Detention basins

Description: Detention basins are surface storage basins or facilities that provide flow control through attenuation of stormwater runoff. They can also facilitate some settling of particulate pollutants. Detention basins are normally dry and in certain situations the land may also function as a recreational facility.

The bottom and side slopes of the basin should be carefully prepared to ensure that they are structurally sound. The preparation should also ensure that the basin will satisfactorily retain the surface water runoff without significant erosion damage.

Backfilling against inlet and outlet structures needs to be controlled so as to minimise settlement and erosion. The soils used to finish the side slopes need to be suitably fertile, porous and of sufficient depth to ensure healthy vegetation growth. If an impermeable liner is used, care should be taken to ensure that it is not damaged during construction.

During the SUDS establishment phase, runoff from bare soils should be minimised. For example:

a) Green cover on slopes should be rapidly established.

b) Base-of-slope trenches should be introduced to retain the inevitable runoff sediments.

c) Construction should be timed to avoid autumn and winter when high runoff rates are to be expected.

Detention basins may be used to manage construction runoff and trap construction sediments, providing they are fully rehabilitated to original design formation levels prior to handover.

Implementation of the CDM Regulations (DETR, 1994) and generic health and safety criteria is important.

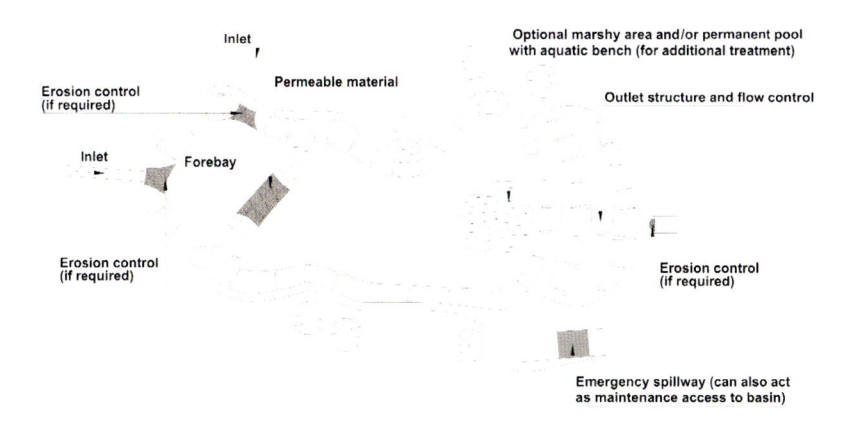

Figure 11.12 *A detention basin schematic*

11.14 Ponds

Description: Ponds can provide both stormwater attenuation and treatment. They are designed to support emergent and submerged aquatic vegetation along their shoreline. Runoff from each rain event is detained and treated in the pool. The retention time promotes pollutant removal through sedimentation and the opportunity for biological uptake mechanisms to reduce nutrient concentrations.

The bottom and side slopes of the pond, including any benches, should be carefully prepared to ensure that they are structurally sound. The preparation should also ensure that the basin will satisfactorily retain the surface water runoff without significant erosion damage.

Backfilling against inlet and outlet structures needs to be controlled so as to minimise settlement and erosion. The soils used to finish the side slopes of the pond above the retained level need to be suitably fertile, porous and of sufficient depth to ensure healthy vegetation growth. If an impermeable liner is used, care should be taken to ensure that it is not damaged during construction.

During the SUDS establishment phase, runoff from bare soils should be minimised. For example:

(a) Green cover on slopes should be rapidly established.
(b) Base-of-slope trenches should be introduced to retain the inevitable runoff sediments.
(c) Construction should be timed to avoid autumn and winter when high runoff rates are to be expected.

Ponds can be used to manage construction runoff and trap construction sediments, providing they are fully rehabilitated to original design formation levels prior to handover. It is recommended that planting schemes are implemented once rehabilitation measures have been carried out.

Implementation of the CDM Regulations (DETR, 1994) and generic health and safety criteria is important.

Figure 11.13 *A pond under construction*

11.15 Wetlands

Description: Wetlands provide both stormwater attenuation and treatment. They comprise shallow ponds and marshy areas, covered almost entirely in aquatic vegetation. Wetlands detain flows for an extended period to allow sediments to settle, and to remove contaminants by facilitating adhesion to vegetation and aerobic decomposition. They also provide significant ecological benefits.

The soils used to finish the side slopes of the wetland above the retained level need to be suitably fertile, porous and of sufficient depth to ensure healthy vegetation growth. If an impermeable liner is used, care should be taken to ensure that it is not damaged during construction.

The guidance provided for ponds (see previous section) should be followed for wetlands, although their use for the management of construction runoff is not recommended. Implementation of the CDM Regulations (DETR, 1994) and generic health and safety criteria is important.

Figure 11.14   *A wetland after initial planting*

References 12

BRE (1991)
Digest 365: Soakaway Design
Buildings Research Establishment, UK

COPPIN, N J and RICHARDS, I G (eds) (1990)
Use of vegetation in civil engineering
B10, CIRIA, London

DETR (1999)
Water Supply (Water Fittings) Regulations
Department of Environment, Transport and the Regions, HMSO, London
http://www.opsi.gov.uk/si/si1999/19991892.htm

Environment Agency/Scottish Environmental Protection Agency (Undated)
Pollution Prevention Guidelines
http://www.environment-agency.gov.uk/business/444251/444731/ppg/?version=1&lang=_e

HEWLETT H W M, BOORMAN L A and BRAMLEY M E (1987)
Design of reinforced grass waterways
R116, CIRIA, London

HIGHWAYS AGENCY (1996)
Design Manual for Roads and Bridges: Surface and sub-surface drainage systems for highways, Volume 4, Section 2, Part 3, HD/33/96
HMSO, London

HIGHWAYS AGENCY (1998)
Manual of contract documents for highway works. Volume 1: Specification for highway works
HMSO, London

MASTERS-WILLIAMS H, et al (2001)
Control of water pollution from construction sites. Guidance for consultants and contractors
C532, CIRIA, London

CIRIA C698

New Jersey Department of Environmental Protection (2000)
Manual for New Jersey: best management practices for control of nonpoint source pollution from stormwaters
New Jersey Department of Environmental Protection, Trenton, NJ

SHAFFER P, ELLIOTT C, REED J, HOLMES J and WARD M (2004)
Model agreements for sustainable water management systems. Model agreement for rainwater and greywater use systems
C626, CIRIA, London

WOODS BALLARD, B *et al*, (2006)
SUDS Manual – Guidance on design and construction,
C697, CIRIA, London.

WRc (1998)
Civil Engineering Specification for the Water Industry (CESWI)
5th Edition. HR Wallingford

BRITISH STANDARDS
BS 7533-3 *Code of practice for laying precast concrete paving blocks and clay pavers for flexible pavements.*

Appendix 1

Erosion control

Erosion control is needed to limit the amount and rate of erosion occurring on disturbed areas. Erosion of SUDS techniques will reduce their effectiveness, and add to the silt load that any other drainage feature downstream will have to deal with. Erosion controls are surface treatments that stabilise soil exposed by excavation or grading.

The objectives for erosion control during construction include:

- Conducting all land disturbing activities in a manner that reduces soil erosion, sediment movement and deposition off-site.
- Schedule construction activities to minimise the total amount of soil exposed at any given time to reduce the period of accelerated soil erosion.
- Establish temporary or permanent cover on areas that have been disturbed as soon as possible after final grading is completed.
- Design and construct all temporary or permanent facilities for the conveyance of water around, through, or from the disturbed area to limit the flow of water to non-erosive velocities.
- Remove sediment caused by accelerated soil erosion from surface runoff water before it leaves the site.
- Stabilise all areas of land disturbance with permanent vegetative cover as soon as possible.

Points to consider:

- Permanent or temporary soil surface stabilisation should be considered for application to disturbed areas and soil stockpiles as soon as possible after final grade is reached on any portion of the site. Soil surface stabilisation should also be considered for disturbed areas that may not be at final grade but will remain undisturbed for more than 60 days.
- A viable vegetative cover should be established within one year on all disturbed areas and soil stockpiles not otherwise permanently stabilised. Vegetation is not considered established until a ground cover is achieved which is sufficiently mature to control soil erosion and can survive moderate runoff events.
- Roads and other hard standings should be covered as early as possible with the appropriate aggregate sub-base where this is specified as part of the pavement.

- Soil stockpiles expected to be in place longer than 60 days should be seeded with a temporary grass cover after completion of stockpile construction. If stockpiles are located within 30 metres of a watercourse, additional sediment controls, such as a diversion ditch or silt fence, should be provided.

- Properties and roadways adjacent to a construction site should be protected from eroded sediment being transported on to them. Whenever construction vehicles enter onto paved roads, provisions should be made to prevent the transport of sediment (mud and dirt) by vehicles tracking onto the paved surface. Whenever sediment is transported onto a public road, regardless of the size of the site, the roads should be cleaned at least daily.

- Temporary diversion ditches should be considered above disturbed areas and may be discharged to a permanent or temporary channel. Diversion ditches located mid-slope on a disturbed area or at the base of a disturbed area should discharge to a sediment trap or basin.

Erosion protection techniques

A number of erosion protection techniques can be used, such as:

- **Vegetation** helps protect areas downstream by decreasing the runoff velocity.
- **Geotextiles** and erosion control fabrics reinforce the soil structure allowing faster run-off before the particle stripping process takes place.
- **Reinforced grass** (consists of plastic moulds which are placed in the soil and allow grass to grow though them) has the benefit of offering early erosion protection as well as protecting the grass areas from traffic loading.
- **Gravel trenches** can be located upstream of the exposed land. They intercept runoff flow that then enters a perforated pipe system to an outfall or infiltrate into the ground. However, because they are usually sacrificial in nature, these systems can be relatively expensive to install for short duration periods. (If such a system is being installed as part of the final SUDS solution for a site then it should not be used for construction run-off, because heavy sediment loads during construction will reduce its design life).
- **Flat sites** or slack gradients within a site will help reduce the velocity of the runoff.

- **Impermeable area run-off** should not be allowed to flow directly over areas of exposed ground. Run-off from these areas should enter a sewer system, flow over a grass/vegetation area, be diverted around, and intercepted by a gravel trench or close-ended ditch.

Further guidance is provided in CIRIA publications R116 (CIRIA, 1996a) and B10 (CIRIA, 1990).

2 Appendix

Sediment control

Sediment entrapment facilities are necessary to reduce sediment discharges to downstream properties and receiving waters, by directing flows appropriately and filtering out sediment.

Temporary sediment entrapment facilities include straw bale barriers, geotextile silt fences, sediment basins (including temporary SUDS networks which can be landscaped or redeveloped on completion and subsequent commissioning of the post construction SUDS), grass margins or existing grass cover. The type of sediment entrapment facility to be used depends on the catchment area and site slope. The table below summarises the recommended maximum catchment areas, slope lengths and slopes for straw bale barriers and geotextile silt fences.

All runoff leaving a disturbed area should pass through a sediment entrapment facility before it exits the site and flows downstream.

Sediment entrapment facility limitations

	Allowable maximum limits		
Sediment control facility	Drainage catchment area (hectares)	Drainage catchment slope length (m)	Drainage catchment slope gradient
Straw bale barrier or silt fence	0.6-1.2 per 100 linear metres	50	1:2 (50%)

Points to consider:

- Some opportunities may be afforded by existing grass cover or the use of grass margins around stripped soil areas to intercept and filter runoff.
- Consider establishing a temporary SUDS network for site drainage during the construction period (eg a swale adjacent to a filter trench or permeable surface, temporary ponds and/or detention basins).
- Consider diverting first phase construction runoff onto undeveloped land away from drainage systems.
- Straw bale barriers or silt fences may be used for small sites. When the catchment area is greater than that allowed for straw bale barriers or silt fences, runoff should be collected in diversion ditches and routed through temporary sediment basins.

- Straw bales can be placed at the base of a slope to act as a sediment barrier. These are not recommended for use within a swale or channel. Straw bales are temporary in nature and may only perform for a period of weeks or months. Careful installation and maintenance is necessary to ensure their performance.
- A silt fence is made of a woven synthetic geotextile, and acts to filter runoff. Silt fencing can be placed as a temporary barrier along the contour at the base of a disturbed area, but is not recommended for use in a channel or swale. The material is durable and will last for more than one season if properly installed and maintained. Silt fencing is not intended to be used as a perimeter fence or in areas of concentrated flow. If concentrated flow conditions exist, a more robust filter should be considered.
- Silt barriers can also be temporarily installed in any road gullies of partially constructed roads to prevent sediment movement onto downstream drainage systems or SUDS components.

Glossary

Algae	Simple plants ranging from single cells to large plants.
Amenity	The quality of being pleasant or attractive; agreeableness. A feature that increases attractiveness or value, especially of a piece of property or a geographic location.
Attenuation	Reduction of peak flow and increased duration of a flow event.
Balancing pond	A pond designed to attenuate flows by storing runoff during the storm and releasing it at a controlled rate during and after the storm. The pond always contains water.
Basin	A ground depression acting as a flow control or water treatment structure that is normally dry and has a proper outfall, but is designed to detain stormwater temporarily.
Berm	A mound of earth formed to control the flow of surface water.
Biodiversity	The diversity of plant and animal life in a particular habitat.
Bioretention area	A depressed landscaping area that is allowed to collect runoff so that it percolates through the soil below the area into an underdrain, thereby promoting pollutant removal.
Block paving	Precast concrete or clay – brick-sized, flexible modular paving system.
Buffer	Something that helps to reduce the scale of an impact.
Bund	A barrier, dam, or mound usually formed from earthworks material and used to contain or exclude water (or other liquids) from an area of the site.
Catchment	The area contributing surface water flow to a point on a drainage or river system. Can be divided into sub-catchments.
Chemical oxygen demand (COD)	The measure of the amount of oxygen taken up by chemical oxidation of a substance in solution. Used as a water quality indicator.
Combined sewer	A sewer designed to carry foul sewage and surface runoff in the same pipe.

Construction cycle	The sequence of events or activities carried out in the development of a construction project.
Construction (Design and Management) Regulations (CDM)1994	Construction (Design and Management) Regulations 1994, which emphasise the importance of addressing construction health and safety issues at the design phase of a construction project.
Construction Quality (CQA) Assurance	A documented management system designed to provide adequate confidence that items or services meet contractual requirements and will perform adequately in service. CQA usually includes inspection and testing of installed components and recording the results.
Controlled waters	Waters defined and protected under the Water Resources Act 1991. Any relevant territorial waters that extend seaward for three miles from the baselines, any coastal waters which extend inland from those baselines to the limit of the highest tide or the freshwater limit of any river or watercourse, any enclosed dock which adjoins coastal waters, inland freshwaters, including rivers, watercourses, and ponds and lakes with discharges and ground waters (waters contained in underground strata). For the full definition refer to the Water Resources Act 1991.
Conventional drainage	The traditional method of draining surface water using subsurface pipes and storage tanks.
Conveyance	Movement of water from one location to another.
Curtilage	Land area within property boundaries.
Deposition	Laying down of matter via a natural process.
Detention basin	A vegetated depression that is normally dry except following storm events. Constructed to store water temporarily to attenuate flows. May allow infiltration of water to the ground.
Detention pond/tank	A pond or tank that has a lower outflow than inflow. Often used to prevent flooding.
Dewatering	The removal of groundwater/surface water to lower the water table.

Dry	Free of water under dry weather flow conditions.
Dust	Airborne solid mater up to about 2 mm in size.
Environment	Both the natural environment (air, land, water resources, plant, and animal life) and the habitats in which they live.
Environmental regulators	These include the Environment Agency (in England and Wales), the Scottish Environment Protection Agency, The Environment and Heritage Service in Northern Ireland, and the Department of Public Services in Jersey and Guernsey.
Erosion	The group of natural processes, including weathering, dissolution, abrasion, corrosion, and transportation, by which material is worn away from the earth's surface
Extended detention basin	A detention basin where the runoff is stored beyond the time for attenuation. This provides extra time for natural processes to remove some of the pollutants in the water.
Filter drain	A linear drain consisting of a trench filled with a permeable material, often with a perforated pipe in the base of the trench to assist drainage.
Filter strip	A vegetated area of gently sloping ground designed to drain water evenly off impermeable areas and to filter out silt and other particulates.
Filtration	The act of removing sediment or other particles from a fluid by passing it through a filter.
Forebay	A small basin or pond upstream of the main drainage component with the function of trapping sediment.
Formation level	Surface of an excavation prepared to support a pavement.
Freeboard	Distance between the design water level and the top of a structure, provided as a precautionary safety measure against early system failure.
Geocellular structure	A plastic box structure used in the ground, often to attenuate runoff.
Geogrid	Plastic grid structure used to increase strength of soils or aggregates.

Geomembrane	An impermeable plastic sheet, typically manufactured from polypropylene, high density polyethylene or other geosynthetic material.
Geotextile	A plastic fabric that is permeable.
Green roof	A roof with plants growing on its surface, which contributes to local biodiversity. The vegetated surface provides a degree of retention, attenuation and treatment of rainwater, and promotes evapotranspiration. Sometimes referred to as an alternative roof.
Greywater	Waste water from baths, showers, sinks (kitchen sinks are excluded due to nutrient rich effluent), and domestic appliances before it reaches the sewer (or septic tank sewer).
Groundwater	Water that is below the surface of ground in the saturation zone.
Habitat	The area or environment where an organism or ecological community normally lives or occurs.
Highways Agency	The government agency responsible for strategic highways in England, ie motorways and trunk roads.
Impermeable	Will not allow water to pass through it.
Impermeable surface	An artificial non-porous surface that generates a surface water runoff after rainfall.
Infiltration (to the ground)	The passage of surface water into the ground.
Infiltration basin	A dry basin designed to promote infiltration of surface water to the ground.
Infiltration device	A device specifically designed to aid infiltration of surface water into the ground.
Infiltration trench	A trench, usually filled with permeable granular material, designed to promote infiltration of surface water to the ground.

Model agreement	A legal document that can be completed to form the basis of an agreement between two or more parties regarding the maintenance and operation of sustainable water management systems.
Open water	Clear water surface, ie free from submerged or floating aquatic vegetation.
Pavement	The road or car park surface and underlying structure, usually asphalt, concrete, or blockpaving. Note: the path next to the road for pedestrians (the UK colloquial term of pavement) is the footway.
Permeable pavement	A permeable surface that is paved and drains through voids between solid parts of the pavement.
Permeable surface	A surface that is formed of material that is itself impervious to water but, by virtue of voids formed through the surface, allows infiltration of water to the sub-base through the pattern of voids, for example concrete block paving.
Pervious surface	A surface that allows inflow of rainwater into the underlying construction or soil.
Point source pollution	Pollution that arises from an easily identifiable source, usually an effluent discharge pipe.
Pollution	A change in the physical, chemical, radiological, or biological quality of a resource (air, water or land) caused by man or man's activities that is injurious to existing, intended, or potential uses of the resource.
Pond	Permanently wet depression designed to retain stormwater above the permanent pool and permit settlement of suspended solids and biological removal of pollutants.
Porous surface	A surface that infiltrates water to the sub-base across the entire surface of the material forming the surface, for example grass and gravel surfaces, porous concrete and porous asphalt.
Porous paving	A permeable surface that drains through voids that are integral to the pavement.

Prevention	Site design and management to stop or reduce the occurrence of pollution of impermeable surfaces and to reduce the volume of runoff by reducing impermeable areas.
Rainfall event	A single occurrence of rainfall before and after which there is a dry period that is sufficient to allow its effect on the drainage system to be defined.
Rainwater harvesting or rainwater use system	A system that collects rainwater from where it falls rather than allowing it to drain away. It includes water that is collected within the boundaries of a property, from roofs and surrounding surfaces.
Recycling	Collecting and separating materials from waste and processing them to produce marketable products.
Risk	The chance of an adverse event. The impact of a risk is the combination of the probability of that potential hazard being realised, the severity of the outcome if it is, and the numbers of people exposed to the hazard.
Risk assessment	"A carefully considered judgement" requiring an evaluation of the risk that may arise from the hazards identified, combining the various factors contributing to the risk and then evaluating their significance.
Runoff	Water flow over the ground surface to the drainage system. This occurs if the ground is impermeable, is saturated or rainfall is particularly intense.
Sediments	Sediments are the layers of particles that cover the bottom of water-bodies such as lakes, ponds, rivers, and reservoirs.
Sewer	A pipe or channel taking domestic foul and/or surface water from buildings and associated paths and hard-standings from two or more curtilages and having a proper outfall.
Silt	The generic term for waterborne particles with a grain size of 4-63 μm, ie between clay and sand.
Soakaway	A sub-surface structure into which surface water is conveyed, designed to promote infiltration.

Soil	The terrestrial medium on which many organisms depend, which is a mixture of minerals (produced by chemical, physical and biological weathering of rocks), organic matter, and water. It often has high populations of bacteria, fungi, and animals such as earthworms.
Storm	An occurrence of rainfall, snow, or hail.
Sub-base	A layer of material on the sub-grade that provides a foundation for a pavement surface.
Sub-grade	Material, usually natural *in situ*, but may include capping layer, below formation level of a pavement.
SUDS	Sustainable drainage systems: an approach to surface water management that combines a sequence of management practices and control structures designed to drain surface water in a more sustainable fashion than some conventional techniques.
Sump	A pit that may be lined or unlined and is used to collect water and sediments before being pumped out.
Surface water	Water that appears on the land surface, ie lakes, rivers, streams, standing water, and ponds.
Suspended solids	General term describing suspended material. Used as a water quality indicator.
Swale	A shallow, vegetated channel designed to conduct and retain water, but may also permit infiltration. The vegetation filters particulate matter.
Treatment	Improving the quality of water by physical, chemical and/or biological means.
Void ratio	The ratio of open air space to solid particles in a soil or aggregate.
Vortex flow control	The induction of a spiral/vortex flow of water in a chamber used to control or restrict the flow.
Waste	Any substance or object that the holder discards, intends to discard, or is required to discard.

Wetland   Flooded area in which the water is shallow enough to enable the growth of bottom-rooted plants.

Whole life cost The present day value of total costs of a structure throughout its likely operating life.

Abbreviations

BMP Best Management Practice
BRE Building Research Establishment
BS British Standard
BSI British Standards Institution
BSRIA Building Services Research and Information Association
CDM Construction (Design and Management) Regulations (1994)
EA Environment Agency (England and Wales)
HMSO Her Majesty's Stationery Office
SEPA Scottish Environment Protection Agency
SUDS Sustainable drainage systems
QA Quality Assessment.